RESCUER

HAWKS

ARTWORK AND STORIES
BY
SHERRI LOUISE JONES

THE REALITY OF
EVERY DAY IS A MIRACLE

A long time ago I started writing stories about some of the things that I have noticed or came upon. I call it (The Reality of Every Day is a Miracle). This book has some of the short stories from that book. It also has some short stories from my book (Birds Big and Small). If we look at all of the things that go on in one day, we can find many blessings.

CONTENTS

RESCUER

HAWKS

FAITH

I used to attend to an elder woman who lived in the woods. Almost every time I went there, there would be a hawk on the electric pole right at her driveway entrance. The lady and I had conversations about the land being destroyed. Not long after that when I went there and she said, "There are fish in the stream now." She said that there hadn't been fish in that stream for many years and that the neighbors were putting food in the water. I said, "The tree outside is beautiful". She said, "It's the first time it has bloomed in many years".

It gave us both faith that healing would be done on this earth. Seeing is believing! We were amazed. A few months later she passed on. I went to the funeral service. When people were leaving and heading towards the place where the dinner was, a hawk was appearing.

HAWKS ON A BUILDING

Sometime around 2004, I was out for a walk and saw a red-tailed hawk that was bigger than the average eagle sitting on a building. Another day right after that, I saw another big hawk sitting on the same building. It was not as big as the other one. I stood in the open and watched it. It watched me for a while then flew off of the building and swooped down then passed by me about four feet away, it flew by along the side of me. Then it flew back up and landed about twenty feet away on a light pole. I didn't move and felt real calm as it passed by. Another person at the park saw it and commented about it.

There are many hawks in that area. The building was in a land preserve. It was surprising to see it swoop down and come so close to me. It was a beautiful, graceful sight and feeling. I did not expect that it would fly down by me. It was not afraid of me or me of it. I had a really good feeling when it passes by. It was a very peaceful experience.

A few months before this, I was visiting the same preserve. While walking the trails I had seen something pink and shiny on the ground. I bent down and saw that it was a stone with white and pink crystals on it in the shape of a heart. I wanted to keep it but didn't because it was a land preserve.

HEART HAWKS

February 13, 2012, I was outside standing under a tree. Two red-tailed hawks flew in my direction, they were side by side. When they got close in front of me right above, they split up and both did a half circle going in the opposite direction from each other then disappeared. The pattern that they flew looked like the top shape of a heart. Right then I remembered that it was the day before Valentines Day.

VANISHING HAWKS

When I lived in Windsor, Wisconsin around the year 2000, I kept seeing hawks in a tree by where I lived. They would sometimes vanish, while looking at them. Then sometimes they would fly up by the sun and disappear. Other people had also seen it and were commenting on it. Some say that it is a sign that somebody had passed on.

WARNING HAWK

I was standing in a field with an elder one time. A hawk flew above us and screeched at the same time as we saw somebody hit my parked car with their truck. The car and truck were about 20 feet away from us. It was directly above the truck when it screeched. It flew overhead and screeched at the exact same time as the crash. We had visited that same field another time and I had found some hawk feathers on the ground around that same area. I put them on the *dash of the elders van. They were gone when I went to get them for him. We were alone, so it was a little mystery as to where they went.*

A SIGN FROM THE CREATOR

Around 14 years ago I was traveling from Wisconsin Dells to Madison. The vehicle broke down on the highway just as we arrived in Madison. I was feeling real bad because I had just been to an event that I liked to attend and everyone that I was with had been complaining and were bickering the whole weekend. They all seemed to think that they knew it all. I had a horrible weekend. Then the vehicle broke down. My mind was thinking, "What next." Being physically disabled it was real hard to walk any distance. My mother lived off of the highway where we had broken down. So we headed that way. I started to pray to the creator for help and some kind of a good sign. Then I looked down and saw a bunch of red-tailed hawk feathers. They were all connected and made a fan and they were not very messy. I picked them up and carried them with me, then gave them away after I got home. I knew that I had been blessed. To me they were a special gift, as to give them as a special gift.

HAWK TO THE RESCUE

Eight years ago I had prayed for my friend's property. I asked the creator to protect her, her kids and the property. A couple of days later, she had an argument with a visitor in the same spot. A red-tailed hawk flew down and landed on his head, biffed him up a little bit, then flew off. I do not think that he was hurt but I bet it scared the heck out of him. She didn't know that I had said a prayer in that same spot. She was laughing because the hawk came and protected her. It was within good timing.

They have been known to do this type

of thing at times when they have babies close by. This was in the city and not likely.

FIVE CITY HAWKS

I was driving on East Washington Ave. one day in Madison. I saw five little hawks sitting together on a light pole by a shopping center. It was a very busy intersection. They were all in a row and equally spaced. They were all about the same size and they did not look full grown. I had never seen anything like that before. I have also seen a lot of hawks playing with the crows in the past decade.

BABY HAWK

Around six years ago I told a lady on the telephone that I had been seeing a lot of hawks in the past and I hadn't seen very many where I had just moved to. About five minutes later I saw a baby red-tailed hawk sitting in a tree outside my window about twenty feet away. I went outside and admired it. I had never seen a baby hawk up close before that. It was real cute and adorable. I got a little to close too it. It got scared and flew a few feet away. Then I just stayed back and watched it. It was very exciting.

HAWK STORIES

The same day that I had finished writing about some hawk story experiences, I went to a medical supply office to pick something up. A big red-tailed hawk swooped down in front of my windshield. Then flew up and landed on the sign for the building. This was at the same time that I was turning into the parking lot. It sat on the sign outside of the building for about fifteen minutes. I could see it through the window from where I was at. The receptionist and I were talking about how big it was.

I had frequently seen a hawk that size

at a land preserve not far from there. I had visited with it a few times and am wondering if it was the same one.

NEIGHBOR HAWKS

Many hawks like to be on the poles around here they are close to the highway. There is a land preserve behind where I live and they like to fly from tree to tree whistling all summer. Some areas have paths and walking trails and some areas are fenced in. The favorite pole for many of them was blocked by a fence back in the woods. There are sometimes four or more hawks on that same pole. I had been wishing that I could go to that pole and see what was in the woods there. I have looked at that wooded area quite often wondering about it.

I was out with the dog one day and saw that the fence was bent over. I have lived here for three years. I got excited took the dog inside and went for it. When I got to that pole after wiggling through trees and dips in the ground. I was very excited that I was able to go and see what was there. It looked like a completely different place then what it did from a far behind the fence. I felt good and the exploring was fun. Under the pole was an animal hole in the ground they must have been stalking the hole for small animals. Over to the side was a large brick block. I figured that somebody may have put it there for a place to sit to maybe watch them.

I saw a metal handle to something sticking up out of the ground. I decided to pull on it to see what it was. Nothing happened it was stuck. At first I had thought that maybe it was from a tent. I had seen old camping things lying around in other areas. I started to get a strange feeling then stayed still and look around.

I started to remember and see that this was also fenced away from the preserve area trails. I started to realized then remembered that I was actually on old military land and *a land preserve, things were looking strange. I was told that there used to mines somewhere in those woods and had forgotten about it until then. I saw different little metal things sticking up out of the ground. There are also old burial mounds around the neighborhood. I got the heck out of there. I think that I will just watch those hawks from afar or just the ones that come closer.*

My mind was stuck on that people get lost in those woods and are not supposed to be in any part of the woods or trails during the nighttime. As this being the purpose for the fence. The entrance to the woods is at the other end of the fence. It was daylight and I just wasn't thinking. I got my wish but didn't realize that maybe I was not supposed to be in there until I saw what I wanted to see from my wish.

March 28, 2010 Madison WI.

There is something different about those woods. One day I looked at the trees in that area during a sunset and a big circle of trees were glowing red. No red in the air or on the ground it was just the trees. I was lucky enough to have a camera and took pictures of them. The following night I saw the same trees glowing yellow but was not able to get a picture.

Right after writing that story I decided to smoke a cigarette. A bunch of smoke rings kept forming from the smoke of it all the way until the end of it. I just sat and watched them. I started to feel very peaceful.

UNIDENTIFIED BIRDS

My oldest son and a friend and I, were traveling on the interstate one day. We kept seeing giant birds that looked like a mixture of an eagle and hawk. They looked more like eagles and they were big. They did not all look alike. They were all different colors. He saw more of them then we did. We were confused as to what they were. Every ten miles or so one of us would see some eagle-like bird. The ones that my son was seeing were as big as vultures but looked like eagles. They were all different colors. They didn't look like they were all the same kind of birds. We kept pointing them out. It was only a one hour drive. We saw them both ways, in the morning and late afternoon.

I had decided to call a local raptor society to tell them of all of the different birds that we had been seeing. They didn't know anything about it. They said that they had heard of some condors or osprey and that was all. We have no idea of what any of them were.

THE RETURN OF THE GREAT WHITE BIRD

One day I could hear what had

sounded like an eagle cry and it was very loud. My granddaughter and a neighbor and I had seen a golden eagle out here about a month before this and I was hoping that it had returned. We hear hawks out here all of the time during the summer. I felt drawn to the sound of this bird and the need to go find it. I knew it was real close but could not see it. I followed the noise to a tree. I looked and didn't see it anywhere. After a few minutes it flew out of the tree above me and it was a huge white bird with maybe 4 to 6 darker colored under wing feathers. I saw the back and under body but not the face. It was shaped like an eagle and flew and sounded like one. My automatic thought was that I was seeing a white eagle. It did a circle then disappeared into the sky and blended in with the white clouds. I watched for a couple of minutes for it to come back.

I called a friend and he came over right away and we waited a little bit to see if it would come back. It was nowhere in sight. All we saw were hawks. When I called him, he just happened to be about a half a mile away on the same hwy in the direction that the bird flew. He lives in the next town over in the other direction.

When he was driving away a little red cardinal flew past his windshield. It was funny because, in the past I had told his wife that whenever I go to an event that they put on about world peace, a red cardinal flies past my windshield while driving to it. I told him to tell her about it. I had commented about the cardinals to her in the past. Then found out that she has a big thing for red cardinals. I have read that cardinals are associated with the good energy of the sun. I know that it was a very special day of blessings.

I decided to stake out the big white bird. I got some food for it and got up early in the morning and sat out by that tree for hours waiting its return. Neighbors had said that they had seen it often. They said that it was a light colored large hawk. A few days *later I saw a large light colored blondish white hawk with a few dark colored feathers. I believe it to be the one that they were seeing. The bird that I had seen was more white and bigger. I finally gave up after a few days.*

I felt that the creator had given me a miracle to witness. It was so exciting that it made me cry in a good way. White and albino or black things are considered very holy to many cultures around the world.

I started an investigation on white eagle and hawk sightings. I found that sightings had been made of very large partial albino female red tail hawks. A few had been sighted over the past decade. I could only find one sighting in Wisconsin. Most of them were all white with a little red on the tip of the tails. The bird that I saw had a white tail. I believed that it was an eagle. Without seeing the head, I could not say for sure what it was, just a beautiful big white bird that blended and disappeared like magic in with the clouds.

During the time that I was staking it out, I had been sitting outside baiting it waiting and hoping that it would return with the camera ready. I went inside for a few minutes. One of my sons was visiting had seen it when he left. I was inside and had missed it. He was able to look at it real good. It was sitting on a pole next to that tree and looking at him as he got into his vehicle, then flew away. It was a very big albino hawk that was the size of an eagle and sounded like an eagle. He didn't tell me until right after New Years. He thought that I was outside with it and watching it. It had returned and I missed it.

He and I have witnessed many rare holy bird experiences together. That was why he thought that I was just hanging out with it. I remember in the past him talking about having dreams of a white eagle. In my mind it was some kind of hawk eagle.

It came back a few times at the beginning of this summer. A neighbor had *seen it and confirmed it also as an extremely large albino hawk. It tried to pick up his little dog. My son was also had his little dog with him when he saw it. He was carrying his.*

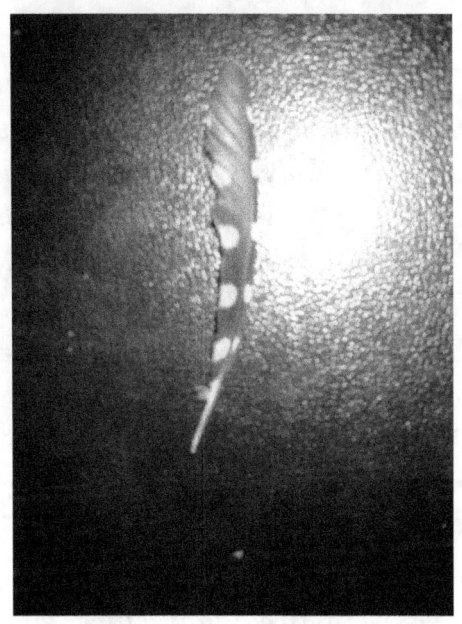

During the time that I was waiting its return, I had found a little black and white polka dot feather. I had also seen a picture of

a friend that I had not seen for a very long time wearing a shirt just like the feather. I gave him the feather. He is a Native American drummer and it was a woodpecker feather. Within many Native American cultures woodpeckers are in relation to the drum. He is Ojibwe!

They were beautiful hawks and we were amazed to the size of them. They are considered very holy birds to many different cultures. One of my nieces told me that she saw a white hawk about a mile away from here. The direction that I saw it fly was north. Within many Native cultures white is the color for the north and some have white animals representing the north. I usually go north during that time of year but was not able to go that year.

I have noticed that since the White Buffalo Miracle was born in Janesville, Wisconsin. Many white birds and animals started to appear all over the world. Many people from around the world and of different cultures have been visiting and praying for them. I have noticed for maybe about seventeen years or more it being more frequent. Also freedom of religion has evolved.

The things that are white or change colors that have what can be changed to colors of white, yellow, red and black are in many Native cultures the colors of the four directions, races and as in we are one around the world, peace unity as one. They are the colors that represent some Native American medicine wheels.

CIRCLING HAWK

I woke up one day to a telephone call from the telephone company saying that they were going to disconnect my service for non payment. It was 8:00 in the morning on a holiday weekend. I told them that I had made my payment and did not owe them anything. The woman said that I had owed $490.00. I *knew that it was not possible. After my conversation with her I called the company many times asking to speak with somebody in charge and got transferred to the same women. Every person that I had talked to from that office told me a different story about what I owed and what needed to be paid and by when. I did not have an itemized statement from them for any of this. I had only two days to make a payment. With it being a holiday there was no time to pay but that day.*

Later that day I was outside and heard a hawk in the sky screeching real loud. It was circling my mail box at the same time that I was collecting my mail. I had received a disconnection notice from another utility company, for a weird bill that I did not owe. It was the same thing, a holiday weekend with no time to pay. I called them and had a similar type of conversation with them as the telephone company earlier in the day.

I had to go to a bill paying company to

make an electronic payment right away. I do not pay my bills online from my own bank account and they wanted it right then. They wanted my bank account numbers and I would not give it to either one of them.

With the telephone company I was harassed by callers from their sales office. I had received three to five calls per day on two different phone lines asking me to take a paticular package deal, claiming that they would save me money. Me telling them, "No. Please do not call back." but they did anyway. The services were not what they said.

It was funny that the hawk was circling my mail box screeching on the same day that I was collecting that mail of false billing charges and was being harassed by two utility companies and being forced to pay them both on that same day. I was lucky that the bill paying service was open.

I recommend to anybody, do not pay

your bills direct from your bank online or respond to any surveys. Go directly to the companies and get something in writing and a receipt or use a bill paying service. You will find out that most of the places will not give you the proper information over the phone.

After I changed telephone services, which was also the provider of my email service. The company called and said that I had been over charged about $300.00 and that there is no record of my bill ever being as high as what I was told. Two one hundred dollar payments were also missing and not documented. So actually I was over charged around $500.00.

They get away with it from many people who do not want to change things as in telephone numbers or email addresses. People also do not want bad credit. They usually threaten that a person will loose these things.

I also had other strange things going

on that day. I walk with a limp. A woman walked up to me and said that Jesus had entered her body and that she had to heal me. She tried to grab my head. I told her no and she kept coming after me anyway. She acted irritated because I said no. As I was walking away from her she tired to grab me from behind. I turned just in time and yelled at her to stop. I did not know her and had never seen her before.

Another woman was supposed to come do some business with me for something and did not show up leaving the work for me. I figured out later that she had been stealing from me. She may have thought that she was caught. Strange things were happening on this day.

What was different about this story is that the hawk flew down and circled the area of just the mail box and myself while screeching. There were no small animals anywhere in sight. I do not know why some hawks will fly close to me.

Every time a hawk flies by me and screeches, it seems to be a time when real strange things are happening or about to happen. They seem as if they are mad about it and are warning me. They fly across the areas where bad things are happening and they screech at the same time. They have been said to be warning messenger birds in the past by many spiritual people.

Many birds are known as messengers and they all seem to have different ways of going about it. I have found that many birds and animals find different ways of communication. I do not know for sure why the hawk circled but it was an odd day of experiences.

This story reminds me of a dream I had about fifteen years ago. I dreamt that skunk was in my mail box. I had an odd feeling about the dream. I went outside and opened my mailbox and found a weird chain letter. It was not delivered by a mail carrier. No Stamp!

30

DIRECTIONS

Many times I have been driving and see hawks on light poles and street signs. They sometimes points their faces in the direction that I needed to go. I find it to be amazing.

ALL THINGS HAVE A PURPOSE

All things on this earth have a purpose. I find a fondness with all of the winged. Many birds drop seeds out of their beaks while flying. Many of the seeds hit the soil then take root and things grow from those seeds.

Females and the earth both give birth, without them there would not be men, children or anything that grows. If we do not take care of the earth everything that grows will be destroyed. The earth has a heartbeat and without that heartbeat we would not be *here. There has to be a balance to stay afloat and we have to stay grounded to the earth in balance. That is why we say that the drum is a heartbeat of mother earth. We all need to keep the water clean too, so that we can keep our bodies, brains, food and the earth clean. It is common sense.*

Children need to learn how to care for one another and the earth. We need to teach them about humanity, kindness and gentleness within their own nature. One of the main things to learn is that we are all equal within creation, discrimination is a sin.

They need to know how to care for the animals and the earth. The future is upon them. We need to teach it as a responsibility with love and respect.

Within a mind of innocence, a child is powerful enough to retain the memory of knowing love power and the reality of it. This is why it is important to remember the innocence of children and to teach them well. I very much appreciate being taught this as a child.

I have written these stories in deep respect to all. For the people who appreciate their love of being a part of this earth our mother and the tree of life, the grandchildren, the trees that grow and sprout roots, branches and leaves of love for generations to come. In hopes of a good future for all living things as we grow on our life's path on to other generations.

About The Author

I am an Interfaith Minister, a preacher of equal rights. I am culturally mixed by heritage (Irish, Native American, English, Scottish, Spanish, French and?) My Father's Mother was Native American and most of my beliefs are Native. I believe in freedom of speech and freedom of religious rights, freedom from all forms of discrimination (race, religion, culture, disability, diversity, age and gender.) We are all one on this earth our mother and we are all created

equal.

May the Creator Bless You!

Sherri L Jones

Understanding
cultrual
differences
is knowing
that
we are all

one.

www.ingramcontent.com/pod-product-compliance
Lightning Source LLC
Chambersburg PA
CBHW060016300526
45794CB00003B/1204